BACKSTAGE BRIGHTON

THEATRE-GOING IN BRIGHTON & HOVE

QueenSpark Books

Published by QueenSpark Books
© QueenSpark Books 2010

QueenSpark is a non-profit-making community publishing and writing organisation
which has helped the people of Brighton & Hove tell their stories since 1972.

QueenSpark Books
Room 207
University of Brighton
10-11 Pavilion Parade
Brighton BN2 1RA
Tel. 01273 571710
www.queensparkbooks.org.uk

ISBN: 978-0-904733-73-0

A catalogue record of this book is available from the British Library.

Typeset in Chaparral Pro and Gill Sans 11/14

 University of Brighton

CONTENTS

ACKNOWLEDGMENTS

Managing Editors
Frank Flood
Sarah Hutchings
John Riches

Writers
Digby Beaumont
Jules Craig
Frank Flood
Barry Hewlett-Davies
Harry Hillery
Jeanne James
Laura Kayne
Matthew Lawson
Rick Martin
Glenn Stevens
Robin Tulley
Lindsey Tydeman

Editors
Isanna Curwen
Tim Earl
Emma Gray
Yvonne Luna
Jacqueline Paizis
Kahn Priestley
Katie Ramsay

Art Director
Nigel French

Designers
Roslyn Cook
Yvonne Luna
Sue Milnthorpe
Umit Ozturk

Cover Design
Matthew Parker
Louise Richardson

Proofreaders
Frank Flood
Kahn Priestley
John Riches

Interviewers
Nicola Benge
Christina Briani
Geraldine Curran
Jeanette Eason
Matthew Ferns
Vicky Heape
Jan Holm
Imogen Lycett-Green
Catherine Page
Julie Singleton
Vaska Trajkovska

Interviewees
Renee Ansell
Peter Chitty
Brian Cunningham
Gordon Dean
Marcia Eason
Len Goldman
Terry Hardy
Shirley Jaffe
June Pamela Marshall
Alwyn Miller
Ray Saxby-Savigear
Pat Shrimpton

Memories

Peter Bailey
Stanley Bates
Debbie Bridge
Geraldine Curran
Ron Ede
Peter Egan
Mike Ford
Bernard Lynn
Rebecca MacMillan
John McGivering
Michael Palmer
Bill Patterson
Bill Richards
Pat Shrimpton
Dorothy Smith
Jack Strutt
John Tatum

Photographs

The Argus
Royal Pavilion and Museums,
    Brighton & Hove
Special Collections,
    Kent University
University of Sussex,
    Special Collections
Michael Coumans
Melita Dennett
Jeanette Eason
Tarik Elmoutawakil
Kristin Henry
Jim Linwood
Noelle McCormack
Tony Mould
Ian Muttoo
Gerald Oxley
Judy Pepper
Jennifer Tonks
Peter Williams

Special Thanks

Donald Auty
Kevin Bacon
Pat Boxall
Fiona Courage
Max Crisfield
Melita Dennett
Clive Dunn
Jane Gallagher (Special Collections,
    University of Kent)
Colin Granger
Jenny Harris
Margaretta Jolly
Marina Kobler
David Lavender
Matthew Lloyd (for permission to
    use material from the website
    www.arthurlloyd.co.uk)
Geoffrey Mead
Anne Morrison
Gerald Oxley
Tom Sawyer
David Sewell
Jennifer Tonks

OVERTURE & BEGINNERS
THEATRE IN BRIGHTON & HOVE

FRANK FLOOD

QUEENSPARK ARCHIVE

National Westminster Bank, Castle Square—believed
to be the site of the very first regular theatre
performances in Brighton during the 1760s
(although the first permanent theatre was built
up the road at 44 North Street in 1774)

L ADIES AND GENTLEMEN, PLEASE TAKE YOUR seats — you are about to be transported by a veritable cornucopia of theatrical delights positively unmatched throughout the seaside conurbations of the known world. Here you will find tales — and, for that matter, a wealth of visual materials — concerning actors, writers, singers, dancers, comedians, prestidigitators, impresarios, architects, assorted chancers and hangers-on. All human life is here — along with the odd elephant and ghost — in a panegyric panorama of Brighton's (and Hove's) finest palaces of performance. We offer you emotion — excitement — romance — suspense — hilarity — all served up with authentic historical backdrops, plenty of business skullduggery, and more than a hint of the sauciness for which our larger-than-life community has long been famous. Roll up, roll up!

What's that I hear you ask, madam? Why did Brighton (and, to a much lesser extent, Hove) become such a hotbed of theatricality in the first place? Well, as with many an interesting history, the bare facts have become tangled in a web of moral, religious and socio-economic forces — to say nothing of personal mythologising, legend and downright untruth. While it's certainly true to say that — following the visits of travelling players from Chichester and possibly elsewhere in the 1760s — the town's first permanent theatre was built by Samuel Paine at 44 North Street in 1774, there's also much evidence of less formal theatrical activity in the taverns and other public spaces of the period.

In addition, patterns of land ownership in Brighton were more fragmented and less bound to the High Church aristocracy than those in Hove, empowering early entrepreneurs to erect increasingly ambitious venues in the town. This activity was encouraged

Clive Dunn on stage

QUEENSPARK ARCHIVE

by the patronage and known tastes of the
Prince Regent, helping to cement the more
secular and 'racy' character of Brighton in
comparison with its western neighbour —
a duality that persists to this day and is
reflected in this volume. The rise of theatricality in Brighton was so pronounced
that by 1800 the *Brighton New Guide* could
state — in a wonderful example of damn-
ing with faint praise — that 'candour must
acknowledge, that the theatrical business
at Brighthelmston is conducted with great
regularity … and that if perfection is not
reached, mediocrity is surpassed.'

But what's that you say, sir? What about
the workers? Well, it was undoubtedly the
case that both the 'legitimate' theatre and
the more select 'saloon entertainments' of
the early-to-mid nineteenth century were
aimed at what writers of the time referred to as 'the
upper ten thousand' — mostly young aristocratic men
with no shortage of either time or money. However, the
Theatres Act of 1843 — with its distinction between
theatres (subject to Lord Chancellor-enforced censor-
ship and a ban on drinking in the auditorium) and other
venues — was an early acknowledgement that the urban
working class now had sufficient income to demand at
least a humbler form of stage entertainment.

Enter, stage left, the music halls — a development
given dual impetus by the opening of the railways from
London to Brighton after 1840. In addition to the labour
force needed to build the lines — a group who demanded
cheap and cheerful entertainment with alcohol in
plentiful supply — the town quickly saw a huge influx
of day-trip visitors from the East End. Theatrical entrepreneurs responded by building or adapting a range of
venues designed to cater for the tourist traffic funneling
from station to seafront down Queens Road and West
Street, as well as more 'downmarket' halls located in the
working-class areas of the town.

The popularity of Brighton's 'variety theatre' and
'music hall' (to use the two most notable terms for this

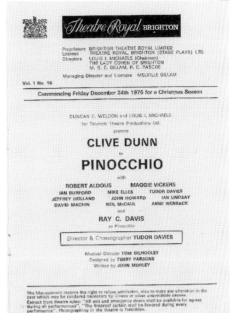

COURTESY OF CLIVE DUNN

3

brand of potent proletarian performance) was sustained well into the twentieth century, and could be seen to have reached a peak with the opening of theatres on both surviving piers — as well as with the rise to national fame of the town's emblematic performer, Max Miller.

At the same time, the railway connection enabled 'legitimate' West End actors to settle in Brighton and Hove while commuting to work in London; it was also instrumental in developing the notion of the 'pre-London run', where shows would be honed via a week's performance (usually at the Theatre Royal) before transferring to the West End. Indeed, it's debatable whether any other British town has had its rail schedules and dining-car menus (kippers!) dictated by the theatrical aristocracy in the way that Laurence Olivier is alleged to have done with the London-to-Brighton service.

While many local theatres became cinemas from the

The Old Steine c.1880s

1910s onwards — a trend exacerbated by the rise of TV in the 1950s — both 'highbrow' and 'populist' stands of stage performance have survived and metamorphosed, encouraged by a generally liberal cultural milieu and by Brighton's somewhat exotic national image. The counter-cultural influences of the sixties and seventies coincided with the emergence of the (initially very mainstream) Brighton Festival to engender a culture where experiment is encouraged and where diverse voices — notably those of the gay community, who have always been at the forefront of local theatre and performance — can be heard.

More recently, a range of companies have colonised new and unusual spaces in order to stage stunning site-specific performances which have redefined what can be meant by the word 'theatre'.

So what about this book then, ladies and gentlemen?

Duke Street Theatre c.1890s. The theatre was located on the northern side of Duke Street, near the clock in the background (where Havana restaurant now stands)

ORIGIN UNKNOWN

In a nutshell, *Backstage Brighton* is a delicious digest — a compelling compendium — of the stories surrounding nearly two dozen of the resort's more notable theatrical and performance venues, together with a range of personal recollections by young and old alike.

We take you from the established theatres at the heart of the city to the smaller and more exotic locales, stopping along the way for some saucy anecdotes and a touch of the great outdoors; and just in case you thought that nostalgia isn't what it used to be, we've also included some of the most fondly-remembered venues where the curtains have closed for the last time. Please take your seats — the performance is about to commence....

CHAPTER 1

CENTRE STAGE

THE CITY CENTRE THEATRES

Theatre Royal 2007

The Theatre Royal
Lindsey Tydeman

Just over two hundred years ago an ambitious project took shape opposite the Prince Regent's new palace in Brighton. Landscaping of the new, improved Pavilion — and building works at William Corden's outrageously luxurious stables and riding school — resulted in a new road where space was available for social and cultural development. Hewitt Cobb, a lawyer and already the owner of a theatre in nearby Duke Street, seized the opportunity. In 1807 he spent an almost ruinously extravagant £12,000 on building a new theatre — one which his nephew would sell in 1866 for just £7,500. But with the Prince, Mrs Fitzherbert and a host of European royalty across the road, Cobb's vision had to reflect his audience's aspirations.

With a capacity of over 1200, the theatre wasn't exclusively for the elite, but social distinctions predominated. Those in the 200 or so seats in the boxes and dress circle enjoyed genteel society, and their proximity to the royal box, and were separated by a gilded grille from the rest of the audience, including those on benches in the gallery.

Nine panels representing 'comedy, tragedy, terpischore (dance), music, love, poetry, geography, astronomy and history' decorated the theatre ceiling. An elegant chandelier hung over the pit and nine others illuminated the auditorium when Charles Kemble opened as Hamlet in the first performance at Brighton's Theatre Royal in June 1807.

Despite its undoubted glamour, making a commercial success of the new theatre would also require careful accounting.

Exterior, Theatre Royal

JIM LINWOOD

For almost fifty years none of its managers lasted longer than eighteen months, and all left it with continuing debts. Then along came Henry John Nye Chart. From a local business family, Chart was an experienced actor with the ambition of forming his own repertory company. With the backing of his father, and his brothers who worked as the theatre company's treasurers for the next 25 years, Henry Chart opened his first season in July 1854 with a successful programme of contemporary and classical plays, and occasional visits from London stars. After his death in May 1876, his widow Ellen resumed her acting career and took over sole management of the theatre.

In originality, marketing skills and sheer ruthlessness, Ellen Nye Chart outshone her husband. She introduced matinee performances in 1883, in particular the two o'clock on Thursdays (later nicknamed the 'flying matinee') — after which the actors and scenery would board a special coach attached to the five-thirty train to be whisked to London for an evening performance. She modelled the annual Christmas pantomime on the famous productions of London's Drury Lane, and the December to February season became the most profitable for the theatre. There was always a special performance for the 1100 inmates and staff of Brighton's workhouse who, in an 1888 address, thanked her for 'the things which you have done for the poor and friendless [that] will be written in letters of gold above your head'.

But Ellen Chart was not all benevolence. She strenuously maintained her monopoly over local commercial drama, regularly intervening to prevent local entrepreneur Fred Ginnett from obtaining a full dramatic licence for stage plays at his Hippodrome in Park Crescent Place. By the time of her death in 1892, Ellen Chart's Theatre Royal had won national renown. Her funeral was one of the grandest Brighton had ever seen, although it is rumoured that she still walks the theatre today — as a friendly grey ghost watching over its fortunes.

The survival of the Theatre Royal in the twentieth century owed much to the vision and commitment of another long-term manager. John Baxter Somerville was a Croydon solicitor lured into local repertory ownership.

COURTESY OF GERALD OXLEY

Theatre Royal Programme
1904

During his 27 years of management (1936–1963), with an energetic mix of concert parties, repertory theatre, West End tours and new work, Baxter steered the theatre through financial difficulties and war-time challenges into a 'golden age' during which the Theatre Royal was established as one of the most important venues in the country.

John Gielgud, Peggy Ashcroft, Margaret Rutherford, Margot Fonteyn, Laurence Olivier, Vivien Leigh, Peter Sellers and Jeremy Brett were some of the stars who performed at the Theatre Royal during this time. Writers whose work featured include Tennessee Williams, Robert Bolt and Terence Rattigan. John Osborne, whose revolutionary new plays would arrive in Brighton immediately after their West End runs, was greeted by the stage carpenter with 'blimey, not you again.'

As he takes it into its third century, current manager John Baldock says of the Theatre Royal, 'it's not a museum.' And sophisticated Brighton audiences continue to function as an accurate gauge of the future success of important new productions.

My memories of the Theatre Royal were 'The Single Gulp' bar (a backstage bar)...with an old barmaid who couldn't resist playing the fruit machine during performances, so always had to wait for a round of applause or a good laugh before she pulled the handle. I have to say that her timing was not that good! — **Stanley Bates**

I played at the Theatre Royal in 1975 with Wilfrid Hyde-White. The play was *A Perfect Gentleman*, which of course Wilfrid was. The problem was that he never learned his lines, so whenever he got into trouble, he'd turn to me and say 'You're so clever, dear boy.... What am I trying to say?' I then said his line for him, he'd then turn to the audience and say 'He's so clever, give him a round of applause'. I never had so many rounds in my life! — **Peter Egan**

Lawrence Dalzell, a West End agent, appeared in a Terence Rattigan play at the Theatre Royal, in a production which turned out very expensively for

Theatre Royal
Programme 1907

Detail of the Dome
entrance doors

NOELLE MCCORMACK

the management. They had to pay out a great deal of
unexpected overtime money to the crew and stage staff.
The play, *Variation on a Theme*, was on the final week
of its provincial tour before it went in to London. The
management had become more and more dissatisfied
with the performance of the young actor playing the
juvenile lead, and decided he had to be replaced before
the show went into the West End.

Not wishing to upset the young man or the morale of
the rest of the cast, auditions for his replacement had to
be done — if not quite in secret, then discreetly — after
the performance each evening. Several actors were tried
out. This meant the cast had to stay on to rehearse with
him — and, of course, they needed the back-up of the
technical crew. This took several hours each evening,
often until three or four o'clock in the morning. Wage

packets for the crew were unexpectedly large that week.

And, after all that, the play did not turn out to be a popular success. — **Barry Hewlett-Davies**

Every Monday my friends and I would go to the Theatre Royal and queue for at least an hour to get a seat up in the gods. We ate our sandwiches in the queue. — **Dorothy Smith**

The Dome Concert Hall, Pavilion Theatre and Corn Exchange
Jeanne James

If you're not sure where your ticket will take you in the complex of theatres around the Dome, this chapter may be useful. Talking to other theatregoers, it was a relief to know that I wasn't the only person who tried to find the Pavilion Theatre in the Corn Exchange in the '80s. Thankfully, the 2001–2 refurbishments have made the complex more beautiful and clearly defined. Contributing to its eclectic style were four inspired architects.

The Dome Concert Hall was once the rotunda stable at the residence of the Prince Regent, built before the Royal Pavilion was fully completed. In 1803, the Pavilion was developed by William Porden. He based his principal design on the Paris Corn Market (Halle au Blé), using yellow brick and in Islamic style. Porden built a riding school alongside, which later became the Corn Exchange. Although it was in use by 1806, the exterior was not finished until 1808. It became known as 'the Dome' in the late 1850s. The Dome is 60ft high and 180ft in diameter: from 1856 until 1864 it was used as cavalry barracks accommodating forty-four horses, with grooms' quarters in circular galleries and entrances on four sides.

The Museum and Library were built in 1867, when Philip Lockwood began converting the Dome into an assembly hall with capacity for 2500 people. He emphasised the Saracenic style in glorious colours, with a dramatic centrepiece chandelier. In 1901–2 the Church Street entrance and the eastern portico were added by Francis May, who also modified the Museum and Library. The Dome was used as a hospital for the Indian Army

Pavilion Theatre

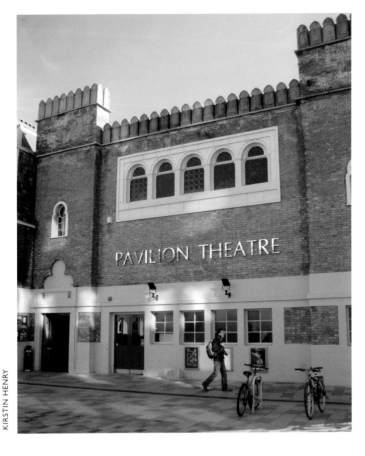

KIRSTIN HENRY

during the First World War.

1934–5 saw a lot of Philip Lockwood's work lost or obscured due to further modifications by Robert Atkinson. An inner ring of columns was removed and a new ceiling and interior were constructed. The building now seated 2102 people. A new balcony was developed and an access road was extended into New Road. Atkinson installed an electric organ, replacing the pipe organ that had been in the Dome since 1870. Douglas Reeves, an organist who made the Dome's concert organ famous in 1936 with *Tuesday Nights at The Dome*, is still remembered by some theatregoers — and by John Mann, who has recently performed shows on the Dome's organ.

Throughout its history the Dome's programme has been an eclectic mix, from early repertoire performances of works by Gilbert and Sullivan, Shakespeare and Cole Porter — and an adaptation of *Hiawatha* that was staged in 1908 as well as in the 1940s! — to Abba's success with

Waterloo in the Eurovision Song Contest in 1974. Many big names have graced the Dome stage: The Rolling Stones, Miles Davis, Courtney Pine, Margot Fonteyn, Jimi Hendrix, the St. Petersburg Ballet Theatre, the London Philharmonic Orchestra, Steven Berkoff, Stomp, and the Kodo Japanese drummers. The Dome has become Brighton's version of the Royal Albert Hall.

The Corn Exchange was once Maria Fitzherberts's stables and, before this, Porden's Riding School. Bought by the town in 1850 as part of the Pavilion estate, it was mainly used for exhibitions and functions. In 1867 lighting was added and the gravel floor replaced with wood. It became known as the Corn Exchange on October 1st 1868, when the corn market transferred there from the King and Queen Inn: the figure by James Woodford of Ceres (goddess of corn) was placed above the canopy of the Church Street entrance in 1934 by Robert Atkinson. Used as an archaeological and geological museum, the hall was hardly altered until the whole complex was refurbished in 2000–2002 — work that included installing a sprung maple floor. Now it has become a versatile venue, hosting shows, exhibitions, thrilling circus events, piano concertos, art fairs, literary discussions and tea dances.

The Pavilion Theatre, with its entrance on New Road, has its fascia slightly set back and was a latecomer to the complex in its current state. Built as a supper room to the Dome with kitchens below, it became the Pavilion Theatre in 1935 when Robert Atkinson made other changes. It still maintained a Moorish exterior, but was more practical than decorative as compared to its earlier companions. You can see the faint join to the turrets of the Dome if you stand on the grass behind the statue of Max Miller. The older yellow brick of the Dome is lighter than the newer brick of the Pavilion. It has a flat floor for a standing audience of around 330, and bleachers seat 200. It is not the most comfortable of the theatres, but it does a good job in giving a platform for new work in dance, performance art and music — as well as the occasional pyrotechnics safety awareness course!

I was involved with Cyril Fletcher's summer show at the Dome in the mid 1960s, where I was employed as a stagehand for the summer season (approximately 12 weeks). It was a fairly large cast, which included Cyril, his wife Betty Astell and his daughter Jill Fletcher. Acts included singers, dancers, a magician and other novelty acts. There was a sketch which involved a pantomime horse, and various members of the cast and stage staff took it in turns to be front or back. The back end had to be fairly strong, as at one stage Cyril actually got on and he was a big fat sod. There was indeed a little dance involved. For playing the horse you were paid an extra £1 a night, but bear in mind this was 45 years ago. I wasn't asked to play the horse very often, as I used to eat a lot of baked beans in those days and there were several complaints from the back end.

'A man may kiss his wife goodbye
The sun may kiss the butterfly
The rich red wine may kiss the glass
But you my friend may kiss my cheek.'
I bet you thought I was going to say arse!
— **Michael Palmer**

Wartime came and not many places opened. But very, very popular in Brighton was *Tuesday Night at The Dome*. It was a sort of little variety show. We had Douglas Reeves, who played the Brighton Dome organ magnificently. His wife Joyce was a singer. It used to be packed, it really was, and it was a really lovely show, and this went on for many years... Later, they'd take the seats out of the Dome and hold dances there; there were a lot of soldiers billeted here. — **June Pamela Marshall**

Komedia

Digby Beaumont & Harry Hillery

Komedia was formed in 1994 by Colin Granger, Dave Lavender and Marina Kobler. Colin and Dave had originally met in the 1960s as students in Wales, and in 1979 they set up a small-scale company called Umbrella Theatre, which "liked poking about in odd corners of European cultural history" and toured a number of off-beat foreign plays as well as shows based on early French and German cabaret. In 1984 they were joined by Marina, who became their stage manager — and later Colin's wife.

The years that followed saw Umbrella travel across Europe absorbing ideas and influences. Denmark in particular provided inspiration, with the *laissez faire* approach flourishing in venues like Café Klaptraet in Copenhagen and the Arts Centre in Odense. In 1988, after much success, Umbrella was temporarily suspended to allow David time to run the Brighton Actors Theatre (formerly Workshop), which staged shows at Brighton's Nightingale Theatre (now Grand Central) until 1990. But in 1991 Umbrella returned refreshed and continued to tour, staging Brighton Festival shows at the Marlborough and Pavilion Theatres to great acclaim.

1993 would prove pivotal for the trio when their search for a venue introduced them to Richard Payne, manager of the Sussex Motor Yacht Club (later the Sussex Arts Club). Richard was impressed by Umbrella's vision and ideas, and quickly joined to complement the team with his proven business skills. Empowered, the search for a venue began in earnest, and it wasn't long before the team found the former Southdown Bus Company social club on Manchester Street — a Grade II listed former 18th century billiards hall and one-time home of British billiard champion John Kentish — which would prove the perfect location.

The Komedia Theatre entered stage left in May 1994 with a Brighton Festival programme of international theatre which would soon become a trademark. On the first night, Malaysian company Wayang Wayang christened the space with a Buddhist blessing and led a delighted audience in an improvised conga line before performing *The Woman in a Tree on the Hill*. Other plays staged that May were an adaptation of Flann O'Brien's book *The Third Policeman* by England's Ridiculusmus Theatre Company, and *Roll-a Pea* by the Polish Wierszalin Company, who conducted their own blessing with vodka. A dream to bring to Brighton performance "with no barrier to understanding" had arrived after a long but fruitful gestation. Although to some the name Komedia implies comedy, it is in fact a union of "company" (or "co"), the state of being together, and "media", implying broad programming. Dave Lavender conceived the idea after seeing a venue called Komedia in Poland.

After the success of the 1994 festival, Komedia established itself as a bastion for international and physical theatre in the region, providing a platform for the likes of Frantic Assembly, Nola Rae, Rejects Revenge, The Right Size, Faulty Optic, League of Gentlemen, Peepolykus and Derevo. The venue also enthralled audiences with music nights such as the legendary *Herbie Flowers' Fez Bar*, broke new ground with children's theatre, and nurtured the careers of household names such as Graham Norton, Harry Hill, Johnny Vegas, Mel and Sue, Armstrong and Miller, Al Murray and Sean Lock. Within four years of opening, the tiny Manchester Street venue was so popular that the company needed to expand.

During the 1960s, town planners had allowed a chunk of old Brighton to be destroyed to make way for a Tesco store in Gardner Street; this closed in the 1980s as supermarkets moved to mega-sites on the outskirts of cities, and the location became a market stall operation of questionable repute. During the 1990s, residents fought to prevent the building becoming a superpub, before Komedia turned it into a multi-space venue in 1998. However, the Tesco connection remains, as Colin Granger explains: "They've moved back into the area, round the corner from us in Jubilee Street. It's where we get our milk!"

In May 2008 Komedia was forced to end theatre programming when £150,000 of Arts Council grant was withdrawn. It currently programmes comedy, music and cabaret; opened another venue in Bath in 2008; and also produces live and broadcast work for the Edinburgh

Festival, leading venues around the country, and the BBC.

'My most memorable night working as front of house was kicking out some drunken football yobs during the interval of a play about football. They were from the opposing team and trying to cause trouble. I was asked by an over-six foot tall burly actor to remove the hooligans — even though I'm only five foot seven — as he was afraid that they might storm the stage. I had a team of door people and the front of house person who helped remove them. One of the hooligans fell down the stairs and tried to punch our female door staff. My biggest effort was to try and remove them without the rest of the audience noticing what we were doing. In a very non-confrontational way I asked the hooligans to follow me into another area, and they were willing, until of course we then asked them to leave, but by then they were well away from the public. The ironic thing that came out of it was I ended up dating the over-six foot actor — seems he liked my management of a bad situation! — **Debbie Bridge**

CHAPTER 2

DOWNSTAGE
THE 'LITTLE' THEATRES

TARIK ELMOUTAWAKIL

The Marlborough Theatre

The Marlborough Theatre and The Nightingale Theatre

Laura Kayne

The Marlborough Theatre, in Princes Street opposite the Royal Pavilion, is thought originally to have housed a ballroom and gambling hall. The theatre's upstairs rooms were used as a hotel in regency days, and there were rumours that the Marlborough doubled as a brothel. It is said that there was once a secret tunnel between the Royal Pavilion and the Marlborough, built so the Prince Regent might discreetly visit ladies of ill repute. Although the official line from the Pavilion is that there is no tunnel to the Marlborough, the basement of the theatre does indeed contain the bricked-up entrance to a tunnel which appears to head in the direction of the Pavilion.

In 1900 the Marlborough was the site of a violent death. The landlord of the pub, Thomas Packham, was tried for the murder of his wife Lucy, who had died of head injuries. Various witnesses testified to Thomas Packham's history of domestic violence, but he countered by alleging that his wife was dirty, idle and known to drink. The all-male jury acquitted Packham of murder but convicted him of manslaughter: he was sentenced to four years in prison. Lucy is still believed to haunt the pub, and the Paranormal Research Society has investigated her presence.

The ground floor of the building is now home to the Marlborough pub, with the theatre located upstairs. The

The Marlborough Theatre

TARIK ELMOUTAWAKIL

Marlborough Little Theatre features a traditional proscenium arch stage and has an audience capacity of 60. It is an intimate and atmospheric space and, in keeping with its colourful and decadent past, the theatre has become a popular venue for Fringe Festival events, alternative cabaret and comedy nights.

The Nightingale Theatre is another pub theatre with an unconventional past. It is situated above the Grand Central pub on the corner of Guildford Street and Surrey Street, close to Brighton Station. It opened in the 1880s, originally as The Railway Hotel, and also served as a brothel and then a theatre. More recently, having stood dark and empty for seven years, the Nightingale Theatre was re-opened in 2004 by Steven Berkoff and Prodigal Productions. It is now known as a flagship venue for new and exciting productions and unconventional theatre.

Both the Marlborough and the Nightingale have long had gay-friendly atmospheres, and a history of organising gay and lesbian events and shows. The Marlborough Little Theatre played host to meetings of the Brighton Campaign for Homosexual Equality in the 1970s and 1980s, with speakers, discussions and social events; while in the 1980s lesbian theatre company Siren produced clever and poignant critiques of women's place in society, often premièring their plays at the Marlborough or the Nightingale, to huge popularity amongst local lesbian audiences.

I came to Brighton in 2003 and took up improv classes on the recommendation of a friend. The classes were run by John Cremer, who soon saw the potential and set up The Mayday Players — now just called The Maydays. We did our very first performance here at the Marlborough in 2004. It went brilliantly. I'll never forget the feeling of getting my first laugh — I got bitten by the bug.

Performing at the Marlborough always feels like coming home, it's got such a cosiness, intimacy and friendliness. It's unique I should think … It has a real old-world charm — the plush curtains, the raised stage — things that many small venues don't have. We have had so many priceless little moments here, it's always fun. **— Rebecca MacMillan — The Maydays (Quotes from *Sussex Life* magazine)**

(Upstairs at) Three and Ten

Upstairs at Three and Ten
Rob Tulley

The old saying that big is not always beautiful can most certainly be applied to Upstairs at Three and Ten. Above a pub tucked away down a small side street in bohemian Kemp Town, the smallest capacity theatre in Brighton is renowned for its cosy, intimate atmosphere.

Formerly based at the nearby Marlborough Pub, the driving force behind Upstairs at Three and Ten's success is Nicola Haydn, an award-winning actress and playwright from Brighton who runs both the venue's comedy night and theatre company Other Place Productions. Their open access policy ensures new work finds a home in Brighton, often from — or prior to — Edinburgh, London, or even international success. Twice winner of the Brighton Fringe Theatre's best venue award, Upstairs at Three and Ten's reputation as an affordable alternative to commercial theatre is growing, with groundbreaking performances in poetry, theatre or comedy by both up-and-coming and established artists. The Theatre Royal it is not, but that is its charm; it does its own thing, and does it very well.

New Venture Theatre

Matthew Lawson

The New Venture Theatre (NVT) is a theatre group, a versatile theatre space and a building full of history — as well as being both a community and an institution.

The NVT was founded in 1947 as The Brighton and Hove Repertory Company. For ten years the company was nomadic, performing in a wide variety of halls and theatres. In 1956 it took a lease on the first floor of Christchurch Schoolrooms in Bedford Place. A 100-seater proscenium arch theatre was then built, with three cosy dressing rooms — furnished with the traditional large mirrors surrounded by bright bulbs — attached. Many shows were staged in this fine old theatre until recently when, due to health & safety legislation, the space had to be closed to the public.

In 1983 the trustees of the company had taken the opportunity to buy the freehold of the whole premises from the Church Commissioners; they promptly added a studio theatre, with flexible seating for up to eighty, to the ground floor of the building. Upon the closing of the old theatre upstairs, this studio has become the principal space in which to host productions.

In the autumn of 1999 the third main room in the building was refurbished: the South Hall now serves as a bar for members and audiences, as well as a cabaret-type venue. For most of the year its walls display high quality framed snapshots of productions from NVT's past — wild actors captured in their natural environment, frozen in moments of anxiety, conflict, adoration and laughter. During the Brighton fringe festival these walls are also used as a gallery for local artwork.

The NVT produces about a play a month, and at any one time there are likely to be three different casts working away within its walls. One group will be just starting out and rehearsing in the South Hall downstairs with fresh scripts in hand; another bunch well into their rehearsal schedule will be in the theatre upstairs, scripts mostly down, running full scenes or sections. A third cast who are approaching showtime will be rehearsing in the downstairs studio itself, partly in costume, stepping over lighting rigs and getting used to props.

However, there always seems to be someone in every cast who has a mild aversion to spending any time alone in the theatre upstairs. There is an alleged ghost up there, still haunting the dressing rooms and the stage. If it's the ghost of an actor, it's likely to be attention-seeking, and to get a kick out of scaring the living...

'I auditioned for my first piece at the NVT on a gorgeous day in spring 2007. It was for the part of Harry Brewer in their July production of Timberlake Wertenbaker's *Our Country's Good*. I'd been aware of the NVT's existence for a few years, but I'd never entered the place before that day. The audition was held upstairs in the old theatre. I remember vividly that hot afternoon when I first entered the theatre. So dark. The theatre was at once delightful and imposing; it smelt of old velvet seating and the pages from a thousand scripts. Something about the place just spoke of homeliness and familiarity — not surprising for a room that had spent the last half-century housing actors and audiences. However, at the same time the darkness and the sheer sense of past in there was almost oppressive. The room was now sadly underused. It seemed to contain the majority of Brighton's dust — in which you could see actual footprints on the stage floor. I remember briefly wondering how old some of those footprints might be. The director Mark Wilson was sat there in the gloom of the front row as I entered the stage to audition under Nature's own followspot: a shaft of dusty sunlight angled down from one of the theatre's old skylight windows. — **Matthew Lawson**

Brighton Little Theatre
Harry Hillery
The Brighton Little Theatre is home to a much-loved amateur company which opened in June 1940 with a production of *Candida* by George Bernard Shaw. The year before, a group of local people from a number of dramatic societies had come together to take over a studio and art gallery tucked away at the end of Clarence Gardens, in a building originally designed as the Clarence

The Brighton Little Theatre

Baptist Chapel. Una Wilson, one of the original members, recalls how with scarce resources and great ingenuity they 'painted and hammered in spare moments' whilst fitting lighting and old cinema seats. Props were borrowed from friends and relatives, and costumes created from rationed remnants; the more elaborate gowns were borrowed from a theatrical costumier called Drury's on the corner of New Road; and during the summer months the blackout presented further problems, as gasping patrons would have to wait until an interval before all the lighting could be switched off and the windows opened to let in fresh air.

The theatre soon built up a regular clientele which at the beginning relied on relatives and friends. This explains how actor Donald Sinden came to give his first stage performance there:

One day he received a phone call from his cousin to say that he (the cousin) had been called up into the RAF, was in the middle of rehearsals at the Little, and would Donald take over his part? Sinden, a teenager, was working locally as an apprentice joiner, building revolving doors in Hove. "Don't be damned silly", he replied (though he and his sister and brother were keen on the theatre, he regarded himself as a philistine).

"No, it's dead easy", said his cousin. "All you have to do is learn some lines and go on." With some misgiving, he took over the part: "It was not as frightening as I expected. I had fallen among friends. I was asked to do another play. And another and another."

One of his performances was seen by a director of Brighton Theatre Royal who was also involved in organising entertainment for the forces. Sinden was offered some work, and from then on he had two jobs. From 8am till 5pm he was a joiner; from 5.30pm till midnight, an actor. "It was a totally schizophrenic existence. I had two accents. My actor's voice would have met with derision at the joinery." From entertaining the troops in Southern England, he went on to seasons at Stratford, the West End, and tremendous international success in British movies. All from a phone call to stand in at Brighton Little Theatre. — **Barry Hewlett-Davies**

Later in life Sinden would return to his roots and become Brighton Little Theatre's president, following in the footsteps of a doyenne of the British stage and screen, Dame Flora Robson, who lived nearby at Wykeham Terrace by the Clock Tower.

Indeed 'little' with just 75 seats, the theatre has a big heart which continues to beat vibrantly thanks to the hard work of 150 volunteers who delight in supporting local talent. Amateur only in name, it also remains fiercely independent, running much like a repertory company with an ambitious programme of ten to twelve productions a year. In November 2002 a Brighton Little Theatre Youth Group was set up to develop the performance potential of young people — the group currently stages two productions a year which form part of the main programme.

CHAPTER 3

UPSTAGE

THE UNIVERSITY THEATRES

The Gardner Arts Centre, newly constructed c.1969

Gardner Arts Centre
Harry Hillery

In 1962 the University of Sussex received a £48,400 grant from the Gulbenkian Foundation to encourage the creative arts both at the university and within the surrounding area. This was to be the starting point for an arts centre at the university, which a few years later would be financed by a £175,000 benefaction from the late T. Lyddon Gardner.

Gardner Arts Centre opened in 1969 with a 482-seat capacity and adaptable space usable for performances, painting and sculpture. Architecturally influenced by the Sussex Downs, the Grade 2 listed brick building by Sir Basil Spence is based on a series of concentric circles, and was originally conceived to demonstrate the essential unity of all art media.

The first play performed at the venue was *Comrade Jacob* by John McGrath, about a band of discharged soldiers from the New Model Army. As symbolic of the late 1960s as a Mary Quant dress, the venue quickly established itself as a beacon of the arts in the South East, and soon attracted the world's most highly respected theatre and dance companies. In later years,

The Gardner Arts Centre, under construction

milestone works by the Featherstonehaughs, Mark Ravenhill, DV8 and Theatre de Complicité meant that audiences were always stimulated. At its peak, the Gardner staged 300 theatre, dance, music, comedy, film and family events every year, with an ethos of cutting edge work, community provision, participation and accessibility. Artistic director Norma Binnie, whose tenure oversaw the venue's halcyon years — and who had thwarted an early closure threat in 1990 — retired in 1998, leaving the venue vibrant, but still embattled by the vagaries of arts funding.

Despite being named 'one of the south coast's most thriving arts centres' by *The Guardian* in 2006, in the following April the Gardner was forced to close. Brighton & Hove City Council withdrew £30,000 of annual grant in November 2006, and the Arts Council withdrew a further £190,000, which proved to be the knockout blow.

However, in April 2009 it was announced that the Gardner Centre would reopen as the Attenborough Centre in 2011–12 to coincide with the university's 50th anniversary celebrations. Renamed to honour former Chancellor, actor and director Lord Richard Attenborough, the new venue hopes to benefit from a total refurbishment costing £4,000,000, providing up to three stages, 500 seats, an exhibition space, café and studios. One can only hope that the vision of Sir Basil Spence and Norma Binnie will once more breathe life into the venue, and resurrect it to its former glory.

Sallis Benney Theatre
Harry Hillery

In 1934 distinguished watercolour artist Ernest Alfred Sallis Benney was appointed Principal of the Brighton School of Art. He arrived with new ideas and an ambition to turn the school into a college with an international reputation. As well as leading innovations in visual arts, Sallis Benney introduced departments in theatrical and cinematographic arts, and also instruction in set design, scene painting, stage lighting, theatrical modelling, wig making and make-up.

Ernest Alfred Sallis Benney died in 1966, but thanks

to him the school continued to grow, and in 1967 a brand new College of Art building was opened on Grand Parade. Designed by Percy Billington, the iconic curved structure comprised a department of fine art, library, refectory, and a hall which would become the focus of theatrical productions.

Director Francis Walker remembers modest beginnings and basic facilities. 'I was asked to give a few mime classes to architectural students. In those days there was a hall with parquet floors and palm plants, and you were hardly allowed to wear shoes. It was all gleaming. No furniture and no stage lighting.'

Francis Walker went on to direct the college theatre workshop which played a significant part in early Brighton International Festivals, staging innovative shows like *Hogarth's England* which used film, music, songs, slides and live commentary. The hall itself was developed and renamed to become the Sallis Benney Theatre.

Nowadays the Sallis Benney Theatre forms part of the University of Brighton and still provides a home for top quality visual and performing arts in the centre of the city. Always at the cutting edge, the venue remains the place to see the more leftfield and innovative artistic ventures from students and the international artistic community. The 272 seat theatre regularly hosts Brighton Festival shows.

Sallis Benney Theatre

TONY MOULD

CHAPTER 4

INTERVAL

SOME THEATRICAL ANECDOTES

RICK MARTIN

On stage at the Grand Theatre, North Road

COURTESY OF JENNIFER TONKS

N ANY BOOK ABOUT THEATRE, THERE HAS TO BE A little diversion into the deliciously naughty realm of gossip and anecdote. So, as a bit of light relief from the factual parts of this book, I would now like to tickle your fancy with a few snippets that I have gleaned from actors and managers who know much more than is good for them about the Brighton theatre scene. Needless to say that where appropriate, names have been omitted to protect the guilty.

This first story was told to me by a pal of mine, a well-known Brighton drag queen and pantomime dame. The anecdote revolves around a Christmas panto in which he starred some years back. The panto was being rehearsed for performance at the Dome. Rehearsals were going well. The drag queen in question (you know who you are) had almost got one of his lines right, which is always a good sign. All of a sudden, the young woman who was playing the principal boy ripped forth with the most enormous example of breaking wind that the legitimate stage has ever witnessed. Apologies flowed like cider on 'skint night' at the Bulldog, and the rehearsal shuddered to a

On stage at the
Grand c.1920s/30s

halt as corpsing spread like wildfire throughout the room. Finally the young lady pulled herself together and asked the director 'Where would you like me to go from?'

'From the fart' came the reply.

Not surprisingly, after that, rehearsals were called off for the day.

I confess I have my doubts about the veracity of this next story, as I seem to remember hearing about it in another context. But I rather enjoyed it, and the person who told it to me seemed convinced that it was legit, so here goes.

The drama apparently unfolded at a small Brighton am-dram theatre a number of years ago. Wherever in the world you are, am-dram always has its share of politics and off-stage drama, and Brighton is no exception. On this occasion the prima donna (probably the one who brings the cakes to committee meetings) stormed off the stage demanding 'Whom do I have to sleep with to get out of this production?'. The exasperated director replied 'The same person you slept with to get the part in the first place.'

The great Marlene Dietrich performed at the Theatre Royal in the sixties. It would undoubtedly have been a great honour for any theatre to host such a world-famous wartime icon. In fact, the management was so concerned about making a good impression on her that they completely refurbished her dressing room.

The iconic lady arrived and, after being shown to her dressing room, immediately asked the stage manager for a scrubbing brush. The manager was mortified that Dietrich thought the dressing room was not up to her expectations. Happily, it turns out that Marlene Dietrich liked to scrub floors as a means of relaxing before a show. Well, to each their own.

This next story was told to me by a friend of mine, the other half of a musical theatre all-rounder who sadly passed away a few years ago. The story revolves around a big show number at the Theatre Royal. In stories of this type, there is always some pressing problem that needs urgently to be solved. The crisis on this occasion was hair gel for the boy dancers. For the first part of the show they needed to have their hair slicked down. Then, after a speedy costume change, the gel had to go. The usual concoctions were considered unsuitable since they would require a lot of washing-out. Finally, one bright spark came up with the innovative idea of using KY jelly, as it was water-based and so would require no major shampooing—just a quick rinse through with water and

The Theatre Royal

MELITA DENNETT

an enthusiastic towel dry. So the production assistant, a young lady fresh out of school, was dispatched to Boots to get the necessary supplies. In the shop, she duly asked for KY jelly. She was presented with tubes of various sizes and asked how much she wanted. Innocently, she replied 'Enough for seventeen men, twice a night for two weeks.' Naivety is wonderful in the young.

Not surprisingly, as an actor myself, there have been things worthy of repeating that have happened to me in my career. So I'll chuck in an anecdote from a production I did some years ago. The play was a comedy and was going particularly well. However, pride comes before a fool (sic.). At one point I was supposed to un-stopper a bottle of wine and pour it. On that fateful night the prop lady had patently been at it with a vengeance, and had pushed the cork too far into the bottle. There was no way I could get it out. For the plot, it was vital that the wine be poured. Finally, at my wits' end, I just forced the cork into the bottle, wedging my finger inside in the process. No amount of frantic yanking helped. It wouldn't budge. Beginning to panic, I improvised lines as I struggled with the stuck digit. All of a sudden my finger popped free of the bottle. I lurched backwards, tripping over the telephone table and taking down a flat in the process. Dazed, and covered in red wine, I stood up, staggered forward, shakily delivered my lines, and poured out what was left of the grape. Secure in the fact that I had successfully fended off disaster, I took an ill-considered step backwards and promptly disappeared from view; I had fallen off the back of the stage. A committed professional to the very end, I popped up, delivered my last few lines, and then dropped down once again from sight. Needless to say, an unsympathetic audience lapped up my misfortune.

Here's a lovely little snippet from a performance of *The Critic* performed by a local am-dram group. On one particular evening, the actor playing Lord Burleigh failed to show up. When told, the stage manager was unperturbed. Over his shoulder, he simply issued the instruction 'get somebody, anybody'.

The 'anybody' was duly found, dressed up and thrust upon the stage, book in hand. His stage direction was 'Enter Lord Burleigh, bows to Dangle, shakes his head and exits.' The hastily found stand-in delivered a sterling performance. He entered, bowed, shook Dangle's head and left the stage pleased with a job well done. I think I might know the actor in question.

Here's one where a local actor wins out over a theatrical big name.

During a tour of *Hamlet*, the great William Charles Macready developed a personal dislike for a Brighton-born actor who was to play the King. The mutual animosity grew steadily over the season until it reached the point where the actor playing the King resolved to get one over on Macready. Armed with a cunning plan, on closing night the King decided to die centre stage instead of his allotted subordinate position upstage; centre stage of course being reserved for Macready's final dramatic moments in the arms of Horatio. During an interminable death scene, with the King increasingly encroaching upon Macready's theatrical territory, the great man was heard to mutter 'Die further up the stage, sir'. His words fell upon deaf ears, the King now prostrate before him. Furious, Macready followed up with an acidic 'Get up and die somewhere else, sir'. Unabashed, our local hero sat bolt upright and retorted 'Now, look here, Macready, I'm the King now and I shall die where I please.'

I close this section with what I consider to be a wonderful anecdote about a visit to Brighton by the late great Sir Henry Irving. And, yes, it is another one about *Hamlet*. According to the story, Irving was performing in a run of the Danish tragedy as part of a tour. His long-time friend and colleague, Compton, was also playing the same venue; the latter opening the evening with a farce called *The Fish Out of Water*. During an after-show dinner party attended by Irving, Compton and entourage, there were the usual mutual toasts of good health. At his turn, Compton rose to acknowledge the appreciation shown by his friends for his performance in what he described as 'that immortal drama, *The Fish Out of Water*.' He went on to express his gratitude to Irving for the 'indefatigable support he has given me in that agreeable little trifle *Hamlet* with which, as you know, we are in the habit of winding up the evening.'

And with that, I wind up this section of the book.

CHAPTER 5

IN THE WINGS
PIER & OPEN-AIR THEATRES

MICHEL COUMANS

The Palace Pier 1985

Out at Sea: The West Pier Theatre and Concert Hall, and The Palace Pier Theatre

Jules Craig

Residents of Brighton and Hove are familiar with the skeleton of the West Pier jutting out of the water, now abandoned and cut off from the shore. For all its decay, many are still drawn to it, enchanted by the stories that wrap an invisible skin around its bones. In stark contrast, the Palace Pier is still very much alive, featuring a different side of seaside life — penny falls, candyfloss and fairground rides. There was a time when they had more in common, flourishing as entertainment centres, boasting an array of live entertainment and variety acts, and both housing vibrant theatres.

The West Pier — designed by Eugenius Birch, and originally called the New Pier to distinguish it from the Chain Pier built in 1823 — took three years to construct, and opened to the public on 6th October 1866. Unlike the Chain Pier with its glorified jetty and landing stage, the New Pier was built for pleasure, promenades and amusements. It was scattered with deckchairs and kiosks, and alive with the music of military bands. In 1893 a large pavilion was erected at the south end of the pier, which was originally used for musical performances and theatre. In 1902 landing stages were built, and a pool created by their perimeters that was used for aquatic entertainment. This was provided by the likes of Professor Reddish, who dived off the pier on his bicycle, and Miss Lonie Webb, who performed a variety of tricks and everyday tasks submerged in three feet of water. Patrons of the pier

West Pier Theatre Programme 1967

West Pier c.1900

West Pier c.1980

were also treated to the delights of the 'oldest living performer and clown', James Doughty, and his performing dog, and were dazzled by the flea circus, which featured duels with genuine steel swords. In 1903 the balcony of the pavilion was extended, the level floors of the auditorium sloped and permanent seats installed, converting it into a theatre for over 1000 people. In 1916 the West Pier was developed further with the addition of a concert hall. Designed by Clayton and Black with white walls and floors in hues of red, it created a feeling of light and space and was described as 'architecture in a holiday mood'. It was also adaptable, and the hall could be cleared for ballroom dancing and roller-skating.

Work began on the New Palace Pier between 1891 and 1899. Intended as a replacement for the Chain Pier, it was also created as a place of leisure, a place to 'see and be seen', and (in contrast to the conventions of its time) a place where the need for a chaperone didn't apply. It opened in 1901 with a large theatre, which was remodelled in 1911 to give it a seating capacity of 1300. In the same year a Bandstand and Winter Gardens were constructed, which have since been converted into the Palace of Fun.

Cover of 1969 issue
of *Sussex Life* (featuring
the Palace Pier)

West Pier Theatre Programme

Historically, there is a sense that the Palace Pier has always been a little more 'whelks and what the butler saw' — for the tourist who has tumbled down the hill towards the sea from the station — whilst the West Pier was more sedate and elite. However, up until the Second World War both pier theatres provided an enormous array of entertainment for all tastes, including drama, comedy, variety and pantomime. Both venues also relied on productions from London-based or touring companies, who received a share of the box-office takings. At the West Pier, companies were obliged to follow the strict rules and regulations that banned any 'costume, look, speech, song or dance...' which was 'indecorous, improper or unsuited for representation'. As competitive money-making ventures, both theatres were obliged to provide programmes which were varied and changed regularly.

In 1908 the West Pier Theatre presented whole weeks dedicated to the works of different playwrights such as Shakespeare and Ibsen. In 1914 the Palace Pier Theatre offered popular operettas by Gilbert and Sullivan, musical comedies such as *The Balkan Princess*, and established works by writers such as Jerome K. Jerome. Over the years many well-known names took to the boards at both theatres, including Ellen Terry, Edith Evans, Fred Karno, Max Miller — and a young Jon Pertwee, who appeared in April 1938 in *Love from a Stranger* and *Candida*. Pantomimes were popular at both theatres.

During the Christmas holidays of 1923, audiences clattered across the walkway of the West Pier to be entertained by the Dorothy Kennard Company performing *Bluebell in Fairyland,* 'a musical dream play in two acts' by Alfred Hicks. This festive treat was a visual and vocal spectacular containing songs such as *A Sense of Humour is a Thing That Isn't Wanted in a King*, and the show offered a stage full of colourful characters (from the 'friendly landlady' to the 'yellow dwarf'), hosts of animals (including rabbits, beetles, kites and sparrows), and a good sprinkling of fairies.

Music and variety shows were well received in the summer seasons, with resident companies such as the Palace Pier Follies, while the Mohawk Minstrels were a

major attraction on the West Pier between 1898 and 1903. Both piers ran summer concert parties before the Second World War including acts such as the Roosters, Frills and Flounces, and the Splinter Company. From 1918 until 1921 there was a permanent orchestra in the West Pier Concert Hall, under the direction of Lyell Taylor. Later, the Concert Hall gained the reputation of being like the Palm Court, where one could enjoy afternoon tea and light music. In the 1950s Ken Lyon and his Novelty Orchestra performed for eight seasons, and the venue hosted a series of old time music halls.

At the height of their success, the pier theatres and the Concert Hall could be mistaken for conventional venues found in any town or city — but according to one audience member who attended performances at both piers, 'you were always aware that you were out at sea, with the water under your feet, and the howl of the wind in the background.' In 1893, when Mrs Albert Taylor performed Christmas stories and fairy tales, she asked her audience to 'step closer to the platform' in order to be

1954 Palace Pier
Theatre Programme

heard over the roaring storm. Theatre crews battled with large sets along narrow walkways, and stagehands at the West Pier Theatre were known to fish through the gaps in the planks in between their cues. Before the 1930s, even amidst all that water, there was the imminent danger of fire, with packed auditoriums teetering on a wooden structure filled with cigarette smoke and gaslight.

At the beginning of the Second World War, both piers were closed to the public. Sections were dismantled and areas fitted with anti-vehicle mines. Even the seats in the West Pier Theatre were booby-trapped. The day the theatres closed, the company of actors at the West Pier Theatre were prevented by armed guards from retrieving their clothes from the dressing room, and at the Palace Pier the seated and expectant audience at the production of *The First Mrs Fraser* had their tickets reimbursed and were sent back to the safety of the land.

In 1946 it was deemed safe to re-open the piers, but the West Pier Theatre never recovered: the ground floor took on a new role as Laughter Land, while the upper floor became the Ocean Restaurant, with nothing but a

Hydrocracker's 2009 production of Joe Orton's *The Erpingham Camp*, performed entirely on Palace Pier

MELITA DENNETT

jukebox for entertainment. A tea room was added to the Concert Hall, which was still used for musical events and variety performances. An ex-Brighton resident recalls going to the Concert Hall to see the variety performer Sandy 'can you hear me, Mother?' Powell. She was late for the show and had to run barefoot along the walkway because her high heels got stuck between the planks.

The Palace Pier Theatre re-opened after the war but, as with many provincial theatres battling with the popularity of radio, cinema and — later — television, it never regained its pre-war glory days. Theatre companies continued to visit, and variety performers and comedians such as Dick Emery, Ronnie Corbett, Tommy Trinder and Jack Tripp performed there. In 1973 the landing stage was demolished, and during a storm a working barge damaged the structure of the theatre, rendering it unsafe. The theatre was dismantled and (allegedly) stored, but never reconstructed.

Now the only remains of the West Pier are starlings and stories, and the theatrical days of the Palace Pier are gone and forgotten, replaced by fairground attractions and amusement arcades. Despite the belief that the Palace Pier theatre could still be in storage somewhere, and the hope for years that the West Pier could be revived and the theatre rebuilt, it seems unlikely that there will be theatres out at sea in Brighton again.

In 2009, Hydrocracker (a Brighton-based theatre company) presented a promenade production of Joe Orton's *Erpingham Camp* on the Palace Pier, with the ghostly silhouette of the West Pier as a backdrop; a reminder of a rich theatrical history now lost at sea.

‘My mother worked for a while as an usherette at the Palace Pier Theatre. Once again we had complimentary tickets. We saw all types of entertainment from pierrots to serious plays. Rather noisy when there was a storm and the sea was rough! — **Dorothy Smith**

I actually had an audition with the Clarkson Rose Summer Show on the Palace Pier in 1958, when I came out of the RAF with ambitions to be a comedian. I think I might have got the job if my mother hadn't stepped in

PALACE PIER BRIGHTON. FINEST PIER IN THE WORLD. 778 COPYRIGHT WARDELL'S

UNKNOWN

The Palace Pier

Palace Pier Theatre
Programme featuring
Dick Emery

THE ROYAL PAVILION AND MUSEUMS, BRIGHTON & HOVE

and demanded far more than the four pounds a week on offer in those days! — **John Tatum**

I was at the Palace Pier Theatre one Saturday night with the lads, when a girl of about 18 came up to me and asked for directions to Rock Gardens. I said I'd walk her up there. The lads went off, and I thought 'I'm in here!' When we got there she said, 'ta for that, love' and went off. I've since realised it was Betty Turpin* (the one who does the hotpots on *Coronation Street*). — **Bill Patterson**

Whilst not as grand as the Theatre Royal, the Palace Pier Theatre in its heyday was embellished with white and gold ornamentation; the seats were blue, very comfortable, and could accommodate a thousand patrons. Although it was situated at the far end of the pier, approximately two thirds of a mile's walk, we saw this as part of the whole theatrical experience. —**Peter Bailey**

---

* Betty Driver, the actress who plays Betty Turpin, was working in Jimmy Hunter's Brighton Follies on the Palace Pier at the time (circa 1937).

Open Air Theatre

Jeanne James

The first recorded open air theatre in Brighton began in 1764 with a travelling troupe of players from Chichester. They performed on the site of the old National Westminster Bank — currently a restaurant — south-west of where the Royal Pavilion buildings would be built, near the South West Gate. A barn was hired and a pit dug — although not truly an open air theatre, it wasn't indoors either! — that contained around 100 people. The players erected rough beams over it, decorated with flowers serving as a roof. It's on record that the Chichester troupe played *The Busy Body* and *The Mock Doctor*, apparent satires of their time.

The upcoming resort of Brighton welcomed theatricals of all sorts and would be the first port of call for street players from everywhere. Adverts in promenade programmes for businesses from London and Yorkshire indicate how far people would come to see performances, and how far Brighton's reputation stretched.

The Promenade Concerts were a mainstay of open air performance in the late 19th century, which usually featured the Aquarium Band with a female vocalist. The tradition is carried on today with performances on the Bandstand organised by Brighton & Hove Council and The Friends of Brighton Bandstand, who led the campaign to save and restore this important part of Brighton's open air performance space.

The Brighton Festival still has Street Theatre as a focus of its entertainment, with the Children's Parade heralding its beginning on the first Saturday in May. In addition, Brighton and Hove is home to buskers all year round.

'When I was about seven, before the war, my father used to take me down along to the seafront to see the *Jack Shepherd Pierrot Show*. We used to stand on the middle part of the walkway and look over the railings, we didn't pay to go and sit down, and I used to like the pierrots. They were in white silk dresses, with pointed hats with black pom-poms, and one used to play a banjo. And there was this funny, big man in a funny hat and a

Michael Aspel dressed as Max Miller at the 2010 summer Max Miller Appreciation Society party

PETER WILLIAMS

highly coloured checked suit, who used to tell jokes that everybody roared with laughter at, but being young, I didn't understand — and he was Max Miller.

My grandfather had a little gift shop where the Concorde Nightclub now is. He sold lemonade and ginger beer: 'Take it away or drink it here!' ... My mother, she ran a little boarding house and used to take in theatricals ... from the D'Oyly Carte Opera, and I think I became word perfect in Gilbert and Sullivan operas. She also had George Formby, and he had his lady friend with a little white dog. She had lots of other stars stay there ... and they were all lovely ... — **June Pamela Marshall**

My brother would perform on the seafront as a punk magician called Shiraz, with an act that was gruesome and entertaining. One of the best buskers I've seen was a lady singing opera by the Pavilion South Gate. She collected a huge crowd, and sang her arias with such passion she moved many of the crowd to tears. The

West Pier Theatre Programme

ladies next to me had tears freely flowing in a very un-English way, commenting to those around how beautiful her voice was. Her boyfriend (we assumed) was in charge of her music, and knelt before her with such love and admiration in his eyes — the tableau was a wonderful piece of drama in itself… the bands and performances on the Bandstand and the open air theatre and flame-throwers of the street — all drawing strangers together — contribute to the spirit of performance that is very special in the City of Brighton & Hove. — **Jeanne James**

Clive Dunn on working in Brighton

Though achieving fame as Corporal Jones in *Dad's Army*, Clive Dunn describes himself as 'a jobbing actor, I was really grateful to be working and to be able to put food on my family's plate'. He performed in Brighton three times … .

In August 1951 Clive was in a revue called *Billy Milton's Party* at the Palace Pier Theatre, which also featured Lionel Blair, Johnny Ladd and Virginia Milton. Most of it was written by Alan Melville*. It did very good business, playing for eight shows over a week (including two matinees: 'if it rained, you had to be prepared to perform a matinee!').

For one sketch Clive sang a number for which he dressed up as a Girl Guide — the chorus went like this:

Clive Dunn on stage

COURTESY OF CLIVE DUNN

'See them marching round and round,
Ring a ring a roses, but they don't fall down,
In all future wars they'll defend our shores,
And give our foes a hiding.

---

* Alan Melville enjoyed great success as a script, song and feature writer and producer in TV and theatre, and lived in Brighton from 1973 until his death in 1983. He wrote for, among many others, Beryl Reid and Dickie Henderson, and he wrote and appeared in the TV show *Raise Your Glasses* with Arthur Askey. He also featured as a panellist on radio's *The Brains Trust*, and in the year of his death Radio 4 ran an *Alan Melville Season* of adaptations of his stage plays.

The Navy need no longer keep the freedom of the seas,
The Army on parade can very safely stand at ease,
And small boy scouts can very safely stay at home and
scrub their knees,
As long as the girls keep guiding.'

Clive also remembers that a rather bored drummer had made a hole in the floor through which he'd fished!

In 1968 Clive played the Emperor of China in *Aladdin* at the Theatre Royal. Yana — a glamorous ballad singer, real name Pamela Guard, who was born in Essex in 1932 and rose to fame on television — played Aladdin, and the show also featured Bernard Bresslaw. People brought their own routines to pantomime, and Clive was asked to do a sketch as Corporal Jones in the Chinese Army. He queried whether the Emperor of China would ever have done that, but was overruled! Clive enjoyed it very much, loving the immediate feedback from the audiences.

During one of the performances, when Connie — Clive's mother — had come to see him, his nose started bleeding. He stuck cotton wool and make-up — '5 and 9' — up his nose, but nothing would halt the blood. The manager bundled Clive into his car and rushed him to the hospital, where they cauterised his nose and then rushed him back to the theatre. After the show, he told Connie what had happened and she said "I thought you were away rather a long time!"

In 1975–76, Clive played Geppetto in a production of *Pinocchio* at the Theatre Royal, for which he also wrote a few songs. In one of the scenes Clive had to dance with the wooden puppet of Pinocchio. However, the person playing Pinocchio — who was a very good dancer — was quite a bit taller and so towered over Geppetto, who had supposedly created him! Nevertheless, the show ran for 4–5 weeks and played to good houses.

CHAPTER 6

CURTAIN

FAMOUS THEATRES OF YESTERYEAR

SPECIAL COLLECTIONS, KENT UNIVERSITY

Andrew Melville II as Corder, probably in
The Murder of Maria Marten in the Red Barn

The Grand Theatre

Glenn Stevens

On Thursday 1st June 1961, a fire ripped through 46 North Road, destroying what had for the previous four years been used as a furniture factory. However, the building also had a more glamorous past as one of Brighton's most popular theatres, hosting productions to rival those in London.

Back in 1891, successful showman Fred Ginnett embarked on bringing the biggest permanent circus structure to Brighton town. The site was ideal. Ginnett knew that, being close to the train station and a stone's throw from the sea, it would bring in the London crowd — seeking sun, sea and entertainment.

An amazing buzz was felt on the opening night, with the promise of some truly spectacular acts. These included performers from Ginnett's London, Glasgow and Belfast circuses, along with a collection of horses, elephants, lions, tigers, stags — and even a parachuting monkey. However, Ginnett's crowning glory was the water extravaganza, for which the centre of the forty-two foot by sixty foot circus ring was lowered and, within

The Grand Theatre

thirty seconds, 25,000 gallons of water poured into the centre. In a minute, the space was filled with swimmers, a steamboat, a rowing boat — plus a few ducks and geese. Ginnett's Hippodrome Circus would run for another three years, before it was sold to make way for a new theatre.

After extensive modernisation, the doors of the Eden Theatre were opened to an enthusiastic public on the 10th September 1894.

'The evening of September 10th, 1894, a vast concourse of people is surging — en-masse outside the newly constructed ornate Eden Theatre — presenting the popular London melodrama *Hoodman Blind*. I, aged 15, having arrived early, am one of the first to gallop up the stairs and secure a front seat. In less than 20 minutes the stalls are sweltering, the pit perspiring, the circle choking and the gallery gasping, so literally packed is the theatre. — **Dick Milton**, actor (***Brighton Herald***, **28th December 1957**)

As well as the many melodramas that were performed

The Queen of Hearts at The Grand Theatre during the 1929/30 season. Andrew Melville II is amongst the actors on the stage. Also featured are Sam Mayo, Beryl Riggs, Bert Elmore and Tessie O'Shea

SPECIAL COLLECTIONS, KENT UNIVERSITY

Andrew Melville II as
Con in *The Shaughraun*

on the stage, one evening in 1896 the Eden found itself engulfed in a real drama when the theatre caught fire. Due to the quick response from the fire brigade, and the fact that the building was accessible from all sides, minimal damage was incurred. After repairs, the Eden would continue to run under that name for another eight years until 1904, when it was renamed the Grand.

Although the name changed, the entertainment was kept the same, with a mixture of melodramas, comedies and plays. The Grand would continue to be one of Brighton's most popular theatres, running in direct competition with the Theatre Royal — especially around panto season. The Grand could guarantee that throughout December and January audiences would flock to see their extravagant productions, with their dazzling stage design and sumptuous costumes. Shows included *Cinderella, Little Red Riding Hood, The Forty Thieves* and *Robinson Crusoe*.

In 1922, the Grand welcomed its new proprietor, Andrew Melville. Andrew and his older brothers Walter and Frederick were collectively known as 'the three musketeers of melodrama'. Together they pooled their vast theatre experience by writing or adapting many of the shows, ensuring that the popularity of the Grand would long continue. These shows included *A Girl's Cross Roads* (written by Walter) and *The Bad Girl of the Family* (written by Frederick). Meanwhile, Andrew appeared in many of the productions, taking the leading role in the opening performance of *Robespierre or The Reign of Terror* — a retelling of the French Revolution. The programme promised a working guillotine, buckets of blood and a cast of over 300. Andrew Melville garnered a loyal following, and received rave reviews and stacks of fan letters for his acting. However, it was his role as the demon barber in *Sweeney Todd* that really had the audiences standing on their feet. Each night the audience would yell Sweeney's catchphrase, 'I'll polish him off', every time Sweeney disposed of his victim via the tilting chair. Andrew's memory is honoured by Brighton & Hove Bus and Coach Company, as his name is painted across one of the 49 buses.

With the departure of Andrew Melville in 1930, the Grand was transformed into a cinema, opening in 1931 and showing double-bill films. However, the Grand Cinema closed in 1940 and reopened in July 1941 as a venue for live entertainment, presenting mainly 'variety style' shows twice daily. Many famous faces took to the Grand's stage once more, including original 'cheeky chappie' Max Miller, Frankie Howerd, Tommy Cooper, Frankie Vaughan, Arthur English, Max Wall, Terry Scott, Norman Wisdom and Brenda Bruce, as well as a young Julie Andrews and the up-and-coming Petula Clark.

For a certain Brighton resident, one variety act left him shaking in his seat:

When I was about six or seven, my granddad took me to the Grand. We were right up in the gods, but we still had a great view. There were a host of acts, but the one that has stayed with me was when a man came onstage with a gorilla secured by a collar and chain. Next thing I knew, the gorilla broke free from his chains and started to run amok. He jumped off the stage; everyone was screaming. Then the gorilla started to climb up the side to the first circle and ran amongst the audience. He then climbed up to where me and my granddad were sitting at the very top and ran around the seats. I kept my head hidden until I was told it had run off. Moments later the gorilla appeared back on the stage, pulled off his mask and took a bow! — **Ron Ede**

For all those who remember the many acts that appeared on the stage, there are also several who recall the ghostly goings-on when the Grand's theatre doors were locked. For instance, some swear to have heard the ethereal strains of *Take Me Back to Dear Old Blighty* when the band pit was empty — this particular 'haunting' was linked to a young soldier who had hung himself at the back of the stage. Others spoke of the fifteen seats in the second row of the gods thumping down one after the other; and two cleaners reported seeing a young woman dressed in her bridal gown, carrying a beautiful bouquet of flowers.

By the mid 1950s, the Grand's reputation as 'the place to go' was beginning to fade. In response, the onstage repertoire became more risqué:

Mum sent me and Dad off to the Grand, to get us out from under her and my newborn sister's feet. I remember watching this very pretty lady doing a dance with red balloons and she kept popping them all, until she was left with just one. On the way out we were each given a postcard. When I got home, I showed Mum the postcard and she wasn't very happy. The dancer had been Gypsy Rose Lee! I wasn't allowed to go back to the Grand after that. — **June Pamela Marshall**

After sixty-six years of entertaining Brighton's residents and visitors, the Grand finally shut its doors in February 1955. Between 1957 and 1961, it became Funnell's Furniture Warehouse. Four years later, another fire would take hold of the building — but this time it was beyond saving. Shortly after, it was pulled down to make way for the less elegant concrete block now known as Gresham House. However, mention the Grand Theatre to those who remember its majestic facade and their eyes always light up.

The Grand was cheaper and more working-class than the Theatre Royal. You could get a seat and entertainment for about a shilling. There were about 300 seats, and there were some real characters playing there, like Max Miller. The most expensive seat was one and six, but up in the gallery used to be ninepence. All the yobs used to go up there because it was so cheap. They used to throw sweet wrappers and everything down on people. — **Bill Richards**

In the 1950s, the sewing machine company I worked for got a call that the Grand needed someone to repair a sewing machine and I was sent along. They took me up to a sort of greenhouse on the roof. Inside was a mess of costumes and paraphernalia. I was behind the machine working when the door opened and a group of dancing girls came in. A voice called out and the girls started to chat and strip off. I was so embarrassed I made myself small, behind the huge machine, and nobody noticed me. After about five minutes the voice called out again, and they all left, leaving me to carry on with my work... — **Bernard Lynn**

In the 1950s my mate Derek Whitaker got a job backstage as a prop man. I was 15 and he was 17. He met Joan Rhodes, a vaudeville strong woman — she was very glamorous and could tear phone books in half. My mates and I used to try and sneak in and see the naked ladies who stood like statues on the stage. We couldn't believe our eyes, as there was nothing like that around — but they were not allowed to move, otherwise it was considered indecent. — **Mike Ford**

There used to be a busker outside the Grand who sang and danced. He often wore a sailor's collar and sang in a high-pitched voice (not very well) with a chorus line of "Bobbing up and down like this", whereupon he'd 'bob up and down' by the line of people queuing to get in! — **Pat Shrimpton**

The Alhambra
Harry Hillery
The Brighton Alhambra, one of a splendid throng of new buildings on Kings Road, opened on 29th October 1888. It was named, like many theatres of its time, after the celebrated Alhambra Palace in Granada, Spain — which gave an immediate suggestion of the exotic. Situated on the seafront close to the West Pier and the Grand Hotel, the theatre was ideally placed to serve Brighton's burgeoning population and 250,000 yearly visitors.

The narrow four-storey frontage, once a modest house on the corner of Great Russell Street, belied the scale of the auditorium which sat behind on the site of the old Whitehall Livery Stables. Once through the entrance,

THE ROYAL PAVILION AND MUSEUMS, BRIGHTON & HOVE

Alhambra programmes

patrons would gasp in awe at an interior packed with 2,000 violet, velvet-cushioned seats. There were French Renaissance decorations in cream, rose and gold, and drapery of peacock blue, all lit by three giant clusters of electric lamps. The venue soon became the toast of the town, attracting magic acts, jugglers, strong men, wrestlers, mime artists, singers and animal acts. It also attracted great stars like 'Prime Minister of Mirth' George Robey (who ended his days along the coast in Saltdean) and singer Mark Sheridan, who scored hits with the songs *I Do Like to be Beside the Seaside* and the racy *Who Were You With Last Night*?

In 1896, Hove resident George Albert Smith patented a camera and projector system. By the following year, films by the likes of Smith and Georges Méliès were on the bill at the Alhambra. The popularity of the elegant new theatre grew quickly, and in May 1911 the Alhambra

The Alhambra

was purchased by the Entertainment Development Syndicate Ltd. Variety shows continued at the venue until April 1912, when it was reopened by Alderman Edward Geere under the new guise of the Grand Cinema de Luxe (Palladium (Brighton) Ltd).

Frank Matcham, who had been responsible for remodelling the Brighton Ice Rink into the Hippodrome in 1901, was employed to design a lavish interior and an extravagant exterior with balustrades, cupolas, statues, ironwork and a roof that could be opened in hot weather. In April 1935 the cinema was bought by the Odeon group, who reopened it with a new Art Deco façade. Following the opening of the new Odeon in West Street, it was renamed the Palladium in 1937 and remained unchanged until its closure in May 1956. The demolition ball arrived in 1958, but the Kings Road frontage clung on until 1963. The site is now home to the Brighton Centre; one can only hope that something beautiful will return to the site once more.

'I'm walking along the seafront, I'd just been demobbed and this voice says, 'Gordon!'. It was Max Miller. I looked across to that place, the Alhambra, which was the Palladium cinema — it was closed ready to be knocked down. He said, 'You got a minute? I'm going to show you something, come on.'

We went in the side door, down the aisle, round the corner and at the bottom of the staircase, he turned left and there was this big room, all scruffy and dirty. He said, 'Do you know where you are? Give us your hand.' And he took me to the middle of the floor and he said, 'Stand there. This is the stage of the old Alhambra Music Hall. Now you can tell your friends you were centre stage with Max Miller.' We went up an iron staircase to some dressing rooms which were falling to bits. He was looking at it and he was so sad. He said, 'There's more talent looked in here, son, than you'll ever see in your life.' And he read all the names off to me, you know. George so and so, Nelly Wallace, Florrie Ford and I'm listening and I could cry. — **Gordon Dean**

The Imperial Theatre

Laura Kayne

Designed by Samuel Beverley, the Imperial Theatre was opened at the top of North Street in 1940 by Jack Buchanan — who also starred in the opening show, *Top Hat and Tails*. The foundation stones on either side of the entrance were laid by comedy film stars Ralph Lynn and Tom Walls in July 1939.

Originally created as a variety theatre, it had a lavish interior with a late Art Deco feel and seated 1,875 (and audiences could drink and dine at the 'Restaurant Imperial'), but was rarely used for live theatre — although in 1947 performers such as Arthur Askey, Florence Desmond and Babette O'Deal appeared in plays and musicals presented by Jack Hylton or Harold Fielding, such as *Music for the Millions, High Tide* and *1066 and All That*. Instead, the theatre often showed films and, like several other theatrical venues, in 1948 it was developed into a cinema; for a while it occasionally hosted conferences and wrestling bouts, before becoming the Imperial Cinema and then the Essoldo Cinema in 1950.

Imperial Theatre programme advertising *Limelight*, a production by impresario and one-time Hove resident, Blanche Littler (1899–1981). Blanche was married to comedian George Robey

Later still it was used for Bingo, and in 1997 became a bowling alley and then a night club. Although there were plans to restore the building and convert it back to its original use, in 1999 it was demolished. Local residents fought hard to redevelop the site as a theatrical venue, but the decision was made to build commercial property, and the site is now a parade of shops and residential units.

FROM THE PRIVATE COLLECTION OF GERALD OXLEY

'I was in a Noel Coward production there in 1954. It was three or four storeys high, a beautiful theatre, really lovely — and I was deeply sorry that they decided to pull it down. The local government themselves were sorry after because it was such a terrific theatre. Arthur Askey was a big draw, as were Elsie and Doris Waters.— **Ray Saxby-Savigear**

The Imperial Theatre in North Street (near Boots) never really took off. The acoustics weren't very good, so we didn't go there very much. It was too modern…decorated very sparsely and didn't last long, don't know why…you just couldn't hear properly there.— **June Pamela Marshall**

Brighton Hippodrome
Rob Tulley

Brighton venues have always been towards the forefront of innovative entertainment, none more so than the Hippodrome in Middle Street. The building opened in 1887 as Brighton Ice Rink. In 1901, having been enlarged by the architect Frank Matcham, it was renamed Brighton Hippodrome and reopened as a circus. In 1902 it became a variety theatre and continued as such until its closure in 1965.

The policy of the Hippodrome was to offer 'performances of high quality, and respectable entertainment at affordable prices'. This attracted cosmopolitan and family audiences in large numbers, and the Hippodrome regularly hosted audiences of over 3,000 — with one performance on a raked stage being witnessed by 4,500 people. For more than 60 years, skilful management successfully guided the Hippodrome through the changing fashions of old time music hall, vaudeville, and the height of variety theatre. Its resident orchestra, for many years under the direction of the inimitable Sidney Sharpe, played to sell-out houses, and agents scoured

Previous page: The Essoldo cinema (formerly The Imperial Theatre) c.1950

Frederick Eason, Pageboy at Brighton Hippodrome

JEANETTE EASON

61

the world to bring outstanding acts to the theatre. As a 'palace of variety' the Hippodrome became synonymous with some of the finest international acts and home-grown talent.

Established stars such as Buster Keaton, Laurel and Hardy, Laurence Olivier, Gracie Fields, Sammy Davis Junior, The Beatles, The Rolling Stones and Brighton's very own Max Miller performed at the Hippodrome. And many budding acts appeared there in their formative years — names like Max Bygraves, Morecambe and Wise, Shirley Bassey and Frankie Vaughan.

The decline of the variety theatre format, especially in the years after the Second World War, saw the Hippodrome host an increasing number of musicals, concerts and one-act celebrity performances until its closure. From 1967 to 2007 it was in use as a Mecca bingo club, with a reduced seating capacity of 1,400. The building, with its leaded glass exterior canopy and rococo and middle eastern-style interior, featuring onion-domed boxes and plasterwork Brighton dolphins, has been Grade II listed since 1985. The Theatre Trust Guide describes it as 'possibly the finest surviving example' of a circus-variety theatre in Britain. Rumours and hopes that one day the Hippodrome will be restored to its former glory and regain its mantle as a variety theatre *par excellence* never quite go away.

Given the Hippodrome's place in theatre history, it is worth noting that in its early days, in a small house just thirty metres away, a pioneering neighbour worked relentlessly on a project that would pose a serious threat to the future of live entertainment. Today a commemorative plaque on that Middle Street house records: 'In this house William Friese-Green, 1855–1921, carried out his original experiments, which led to a world-wide industry'. That world-wide industry was … the cinema.

There was a circus at the theatre one week and the dock doors that led straight out into the car park were left open one morning to let in some air. The elephant got loose from his tethering rope and decided to have a look around Brighton. It walked out of the dock doors past the stage door and

Brighton Hippodrome
Programme

COURTESY OF THE ARGUS

a large window in the stage doorkeeper's cubby hole. George panicked when he found the elephant gone and asked the stage door keeper if he had seen it pass by. The stage door keeper said he had not noticed it. George screamed at him that he must have noticed it because the animal must have blocked out the f****** daylight as it passed his window. The elephant was eventually found taking a stroll around the lanes and accepting buns from passers by. — **Donald Auty**[*]

On Sunday 2 June 1963 the show [Roy Orbison and The Beatles] arrived at the Brighton Hippodrome. I was, and still am, a big fan of Roy Orbison and had managed to obtain seats in the stalls for me and my future wife Pam to see my hero in the flesh. Middle Street was packed with fans, mostly young girls who had come not to see Roy, but The Beatles.... From the moment they came on stage the girls screamed to such a pitch that I couldn't hear a word they were singing. My memory is of John, Paul and George 'mouthing' into the microphones while

Brighton Hippodrome in its Bingo Hall days

[*] http://www.arthurlloyd.co.uk

Ringo banged away on the drums behind them. It was an unforgettable evening and my only regret is that I didn't keep the tickets or the programme. What would they be worth today? — **Jack Strutt**

On Saturdays I often went to the Hippodrome to see the variety show. Entrance to the gallery promenade was a shilling, and a half pint of Kemp Town brown ale was also a shilling. If you had supper at a café in the arches near the club (egg and chips for one and six) it was a cheap evening out. — **John McGivering**

The Hippodrome had a fabulous pit orchestra which was conducted by the renowned and distinguished Sidney Sharpe and which could turn its hand to any style of music. There was also a very nice bar which sold Watney's Red Barrel. Not as good as real ale, but a name to conjure with in those days. — **John Tatum**

In 1948, when I was sixteen, I joined the Brighton and Hove Operatic Society for their production of *New Moon* at the Hippodrome. I was in the chorus which involved five changes of costumes, ranging from a custody officer to a sailor. The dressing rooms were high up in the wings, so I expended a lot of puff running up and down to change. Fortunately I never missed my

Elephants outside
Brighton Hippodrome

entrance. — **Peter Bailey**

Brighton Hippodrome

My Aunt recalls, probably in the early 50s, taking me
to the Hippodrome to see Alfred Marks in *Ali Baba and
the 40 Thieves*. Every time Alfred Marks came on stage,
presumably as a baddy, I screamed my head off. After
a while, he got so annoyed with me and my bawlings
that he asked my aunt to 'Take that bloody child
out!' — **Geraldine Curran**

Dolphin Theatre
Rob Tulley

Stroll northwards, a few hundred yards past the Theatre
Royal in New Road, and you come to a block of non-
descript contemporary offices on the site of its former
twin theatre, the Dolphin. Originally on the site of the
Dolphin Theatre stood a wine and spirit warehouse
which was converted into a music hall in 1863. Known
as the Oxford Music Hall, it was — like many other
venues in the city — destroyed by fire only four years
later in 1867. The following year it was rebuilt and

renamed Wright's New Oxford Music Hall. This building was to last a bit longer, but closed in 1891 — once again destroyed by fire. Premises next door and space at the rear were then acquired, giving access to Bond Street, and the site was cleared for the building of a new music hall on this enlarged site: the Brighton Empire opened in 1892 and had an ornamental façade 60 feet long, with three storeys of highly decorated scrollwork featuring historic emblems. It had a capacity of 1,400 and most of the best-known music hall artists of the day appeared there, including Albert Chevalier, Eugene Stratton, R.G. Knowles, Dan Leno, Harry Champion, Little Titch, Marie Lloyd and George Robey.

The Brighton Empire was acquired in 1902 by Tom Barrasford, whose northern music hall circuit was based at the Hippodrome in Middle Street, and the venue was renamed The Coliseum when it reopened as a variety theatre in 1909. For a short period it also became known as the Court Picture Palace and was bought by Gaumont

New Road c.1967. The photograph shows The Paris Cinema (formerly The Dolphin Theatre)

THE ROYAL PAVILION AND MUSEUMS, BRIGHTON & HOVE

British as one of a chain of 150 cinemas, showing amongst other features many of Max Miller's films, of which he made fourteen between 1933 and 1942.

It was in 1945 that the building was acquired by John Baxter Somerville, director of the Theatre Royal, and in May 1947 it was reopened and managed by him as the Dolphin Theatre. Remodelled, and with a reduced seating capacity of 850, it was used as a repertory theatre and occasionally for showing films, and was also a regular host to summer shows and pantomimes. Tony Hancock played one of the ugly sisters there in *Cinderella* in 1948–49. In 1952 the theatre was renamed yet again, this time as Her Majesty's, and continued the tradition of its previous incarnation by producing summer shows and pantomime. However, this was short-lived, and after a final performance of *Beauty and the Beast* it closed again on 20th January 1955.

With the demise of variety, the theatre then reopened as the Paris Continental, specialising in foreign films. It continued as a loss-making concern until 2nd March 1962, when it finally closed.

A campaign was launched to try and save the theatre from demolition, supported by many leading actors of the time, including Sir Ralph Richardson, Sir Laurence Olivier and Charles Laughton. There was even a proposal that Brighton Council should buy it for use as the town's museum of costume, but unfortunately this was unsuccessful and the theatre was demolished in 1967. Brighton had lost another part of its theatrical heritage, bringing to a close 104 years of entertainment on the site.

'When I used to go [to The Dolphin] there was an excellent repertory company. When they were disbanding I wrote to the *Argus* saying that I could not understand why they weren't getting sufficient support from the Brighton public as it was the best rep company that I had ever seen. In fact it was the only rep company that I had ever seen at that time. — **Dorothy Smith**

It was a little ordinary theatre … you got wooden seats up in 'the gods' for a shilling or something and you could have tea and biscuits in the

interval. — **June Pamela Marshall**

Brighton Combination
Digby Beaumont

The anti-Vietnam War movement, feminism, Black Power, student activism — the second half of the 1960s was a time of great social unrest. A counterculture had emerged. People were challenging authority and the prevailing conservative norms. They were going to change the world.

Noel Greig, Jenny Harris and Ruth Marks had been friends at university in London. Inspired by radical developments in theatre — especially the first 'Arts Laboratory', an experimental, multi-purpose centre opened in London by American Jim Haynes — Noel, Jenny and Ruth agreed to set up a place of their own somewhere. Deciding on Brighton, as both Jenny and Ruth had spent time in the town as children, they found a venue — a former Victorian schoolhouse located up an alleyway at the south end of West Street (currently out-buildings to number 77), a pebble's throw from Brighton beach — which they acquired for a peppercorn rent. They converted the building themselves, with help from local artists, and opened in early spring 1967 with an all day-all night café, music, shows by visiting companies, a

Brighton Combination Flyer

silkscreen workshop and exhibitions. It was named the Brighton Combination after the 1825 Combination Laws that made it legal for workers to 'combine together' to bargain over wages and working conditions.

'We were demonstrating support for workers,' Jenny Harris explains. 'We set up the place with funds begged, borrowed and probably stolen! We didn't even know about the existence of things like the Arts Council. The theory was that income from the café and ticket sales would fund the art. After about nine months of operation, we were visited by a man who introduced himself as Dennis Andrews from the Arts Council. He had a good look round, saw the show on in the theatre and went away. Then we got a letter offering us a grant of £825. We never applied! Can't imagine that happening today!'

The Combination was a 'black box' theatre: a versatile, flexible space that was constantly reconfigured. In an interview, the late Noel Greig described its day-to-day workings: 'You'd go in in the morning, early, you'd prepare all the food … you'd go and rehearse, and then

Brighton Combination was located in the alley to the right of the Family Leisure Arcade at 76 West Street

those people who weren't in the play would be serving the food in the evening...then we'd do the play and then move everything around and we'd show a film, we had an old projector and we'd show films, radical films, and then that'd finish and we'd turn it into a dance space, and have light shows. This would go on 'til 3 in the morning, we'd have a few joints, go to bed, get up the next day and do it all again!'

In 1971 Noel, Jenny and Ruth were offered a three-year grant to set up and run community action and arts development projects at the Albany Centre in Deptford, London. They accepted, thinking at first they could manage both London and Brighton venues, but soon discovered it was impossible: the Brighton Combination closed that same year.

ENCORE

10 UNUSUAL BRIGHTON & HOVE
THEATRICAL VENUES

FRANK FLOOD

Zap Club Postcard, 1984

1) Brighton Unity Theatre

Located in York Road, this offshoot of the avowedly socialist and anti-fascist Workers' Theatre Movement opened in 1936 with J. B. Priestley's polemical drama *They Came to a City*. Openly at odds with what they described as 'profit-seeking sponsors playing down their cultural aspirations', they were one of over 250 local Unity Theatres opened in the UK in the years leading up to WW2.

2) David Land Arts Centre

This building in Upper Gardner Street — once a school and then a boys' club, now memorably described by a local publication as 'yuppie flats' — saw its rehearsal-and-performance heyday in the 1980s and 1990s as the David Land Arts Centre (later the Ray Tindle Centre). This was where Andrew Lloyd Webber did his preparatory work for shows such as *Evita*, as well as being a studio-theatre space for many emerging local performers of the era.

Iambic Arts Theatre

JUDY PEPPER

3) Iambic Arts Theatre

The graffiti adorning the Regent Street entrance to this 'perfectly built bijou environment' gives some idea of the avowedly esoteric fare on offer within. One of the newer and more fiercely independent venues in the city, Iambic is the brainchild of Emma D'Arcy and is affiliated with Pentameters Theatre in Hampstead. If you like purple and black, you'll like this.

4) Bom-Banes

Is it a restaurant? a cabaret? an art space? a theatre? The truth is that this tiny and eccentric venue in George Street is all of these, and possibly more besides. Jane Bom-Bane and Nick Pynn preside over Belgian cuisine, music, films and (at the last count) two of their own self-written and self-referential musicals, which you can experience while ensconced at a monastery table. Or on the back seat of a car. Honest.

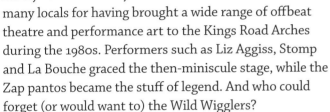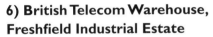

5) The Zap

As well as being one of Brighton's defining music-and-clubbing venues, the Zap — now Digital — is fondly remembered by many locals for having brought a wide range of offbeat theatre and performance art to the Kings Road Arches during the 1980s. Performers such as Liz Aggiss, Stomp and La Bouche graced the then-miniscule stage, while the Zap pantos became the stuff of legend. And who could forget (or would want to) the Wild Wigglers?

Zap Club Flyer, 1984

6) British Telecom Warehouse, Freshfield Industrial Estate

In 1986, this hangar of a building became a suitable space for *The Rail*, an extraordinary early incarnation of what we now know as 'site-specific theatre' by Carbone 14. This Montreal-based theatre company introduced Brighton audiences to the immersive joys of human torches, real rain and a full-sized moving railway in the course of a single evening. Some of us have never been the same since; unlike the venue, which is still a warehouse.

7) Stanmer House

Nowadays, 'site-specific' productions are all the rage — but few have been as haunting as dreamthinkspeak's 2003 piece *Don't Look Back*, which recast the Orpheus-and-Eurydice myth as a journey from the (now closed) Gardner Arts Centre via chauffeur-driven limo to the then-decaying Georgian corridors, anterooms and cellars of Stanmer House. The venue's subsequent rebirth as a posh wedding-and-conference locale merely serves as an ironic counterpoint to the psychic archaeology offered by this memorable performance.

8) Grand Ocean Hotel, Saltdean

And speaking of ironic counterpoints: those who were lucky enough to experience (no other word for it) Frantic Assembly's *Dirty Wonderland* during the 2005 Brighton Festival will be struck by the anodyne nature of the current 'luxury apartment' redevelopment of the Art Deco masterpiece that was once Butlins Saltdean Hotel. By contrast, this Nan Goldin-inspired promenade through desire, debauchery and death made its audience painfully aware of what might lie behind the facade of 'glamour'....

9) Aquarium Colonnade Toilets

Among the many memorable performances witnessed in Brighton conveniences over the decades, perhaps the most theatrically 'legit' and yet determinedly provocative was Semper Fi Theatre's 2004 Brighton Festival staging of Paul Walker's *Ladies and Gents* in the only possible venue for such a title. Anything that could get the Argus critic to write approvingly (if perhaps unintentionally) of 'sight-specific curiosity' in this sort of setting must have been worth spending a penny for.

10) London Road Co-Op

Finally and fittingly, the most acclaimed recent reclamation of 'empty space' in Brighton: dreamthinkspeak's extraordinary 2010 event *Before I Sleep*, in which the spirit of Chekhov comes to the old Co-Op department store complete with snow, deep-sea divers, full-on communist bloc shopping experiences and a real cherry tree. If proof were needed that theatre in Brighton could still surprise after more than two centuries, this was it....